GOD IS IN CONTROL
By
Leonard O. Spurling

Table of Contents

DEDICATION

This book is dedicated to the men who meant so much to me while I was growing up at Moseley Chapel Christian Methodist Episcopal Church and during my ministry. They are Bro. Frazier Dansby, Bro. Brice Else, Bro. Finnis Skinner, Bro. Ray Smith, Bro. Oscar Shamlin, Rev. Dr. Jerome McNeil, (whom I admired), Rev. Dr. Presiding Elder Henry Q. Dickerson, and Bishop Ronald Cunningham, (who was always encouraging and uplifting).

I also want to thank Bishop Marshal Gilmore for believing in me, even when I could not stay focused. And Rev. Willie McAlister for opening his doors to me, reading my material, and his encouragement. God bless you and Michael Lane along with his wife Vanessa, my dear neighbors, who has been a true brother and sister in the Lord. Thank you so much for your support. Love you always. All but four (Gilmore, McAlister, Michael, and Vanessa) of these people are now with the Lord, but they will never be forgotten.

INTRODUCTION

I have been in law enforcement for 40 years and a church pastor for 34 years. I have seen and learned so much about the law itself and how it affects all people in many walks of life, whether they are Black, White, Asian, Hispanic, etc. Whether it affects us negatively or positively, the law affects us all. However, I have also learned that there is one who not only created the law through His word but is above all, works in all, and through all. That is our Lord and Savior, Jesus Christ.

Though some use the law to benefit themselves, God is sovereign, and nothing happens without His control; in other words, evil cannot do anything without God's permission. The proof is in Job 1:12 when the Lord allowed Job to be tested by Satan:

> **The Lord said to Satan, "Very well, then,**
> **everything he (Job) has is in your hands,**
> **but on the man himself do not lay a finger.**
>
> **Job 1:12, NIV**

God gave His permission for Satan to attack Job, and as we can see, Satan could only do what God allowed. This supports the scripture:

And we know that in all things God works for the good of those who love Him, who have been called according to His purpose.

Romans 8:28, NIV

Whatever happens, good or bad, God is working something out, even when there is no clear picture of what God is doing or when it may appear that evil has overcome. God has proven Himself repeatedly that He makes ways out of no ways.

As during the times of Job, God is still the same today. Though we change and at times break promises to Him, God always keeps His promises toward us.

He never leaves us nor forsakes us. He knows what is best for us. For several years, I have had a burning desire to talk not only to our people and our children but also to others about how God is above all things. Others can twist, turn, or bind the Law; however, they cannot twist, turn, or bind God.

No matter how powerful others think they are, no matter what powerful position they are in, God makes the ultimate decision, and God is in charge. The Bible tells us clearly in Psalms 37:1:

Do not fret because of those who do evil or be envious of those who do wrong.

Psalms 37:1, NIV

Some of us see people with some kind of power doing wrong or taking advantage of others through deception, coercion, or exhortation while prospering.

Yet they seem to be getting away with it. When we see this type of behavior, knowing what they are doing is wrong and knowing that it will eventually catch up with them, we somehow come to admire those people, hold them in high esteem, make them our heroes, and soon adopt their character. Soon, we tolerate the very thing that we have fought against; we learn to live with it, and then we adopt the characteristic of the very thing we have fought against.

We as Christians today have become so carnal about how we handle such situations, that it has affected our personal lives.

Some of us think that breaking the law to get ahead is an admirable thing and we accept it as the answer. For some of us, if breaking the law does not work, we become frustrated and blame the system for our mishaps.

This is not to say that the system does not have flaws and will continue to have them, but when we purposely put ourselves in that position of justifiable sin, then the Lord will allow our consequences to catch up with us. Sin is sin, no matter how we try to fix it or dress it up. I had to learn this the hard way and I praise God I did! Despite justifiably accepting sin in my life and trying to cover it up through scripture and at times pulling the race card, God never left me alone. He never gave up on me.

As you read the first chapter, you will see that God had to strip me of my reputation and knock me down to almost nothing to get my attention. I don't call this punishment by any means! I call this correction through His loving grace.

Everything I lost through my own fault, He gave it all back and more when I repented, including a new character and a new relationship. What I truly love about God is no matter how far we stray or where we are in our lives, He will meet us on our levels and bring us back to where we belong in Him.

CHAPTER 1

God is the Ultimate Authority

**Let every soul be in subjection to higher
authority, for there is no authority except by God.**

Romans 13:1, NIV

Today, as we see the breakdown in our society, some of us would assume that the law is corrupt. As popular as this statement may sound to certain groups, it is not the law that is corrupt, but we as the people who interpret the law. According to the books of Exodus. Leviticus, Numbers, and reiterated through Deuteronomy, God created the laws to govern the people and to keep our society from tearing one another apart. Without the law, there would be no peace.

Others who have no conscience of right or wrong will do or act as they please with no concern for how this could affect the lives of others.

Working as a law enforcement officer, I have seen my share of corruption and blatant disregard for the law. I have also seen officials, community leaders, citizens whether rich or poor, black or white, and even those who enforce the laws, such as politicians, certain leaders, and even police officers, bend and twist the laws to fit their personal agendas, intentions, or to use their authority to get certain privileges or to cover up a behavior that is not acceptable for the position. However, again, it does not mean that the law itself is corrupt.

Despite the corruption that we as Christians may see or what we must endure because of the corruption of others, especially those in power, it does not give Christians the right to rebel, disobey the law, or riot against authorities. God has anointed authority, and when we rebel against it or do what is right in our own eyes, we rebel against God! Some would ask, "What if you are dealing with a corrupt leader?"

Well, I'm here to tell you that God will deal with those leaders. The proof is how he dealt with Nebuchadnezzar in Daniel 4. Also, it says in the book of Proverbs,

> **In the Lord's hand, the king's heart is a stream of water that He channels toward all who please Him.**
>
> **Proverbs 21:1, (NIV)**

Some leaders think they have so much control that nothing or no one can touch them. However, they soon learn a very hard lesson that God is in control and has control over them, even when they feel they have the power to do whatever they please. God is sovereign. He is also in control of correction. Believe me, I know because He dealt with me.

At one point, I was one of those officers who needed correction. Although I did not act on most of the behavior traits I was carrying within myself, the Lord saw fit to cleanse my heart by allowing one of those traits to come to the surface. During His correction of me, at first, I thought that God was too harsh.

As years, went by and I grew to understand God and His true character, I realized that what God had done was not punishment. It was discipline through His grace.

He could have continued to let me go and do whatever I pleased, and my troubles could have been worse, but He saw fit to stop me in my tracks. Now, all I can do is praise Him. Because of my actions, the Lord took my badge for about a month and a half. No police or sheriff's department would accept me anywhere, so it seemed. Some departments would say that they wanted to wait until things died down or the smoke cleared. Others were just a flat "no!"

God Establishing His Authority

REALIZING THAT I NEEDED a job very quickly to take care of my family, I turned to Labor Ready and Remedy temp agencies, and the Lord saw fit to send me there. Going to these jobs was not only embarrassing but downright devastating. The people I worked with had the potential of me arresting them for a crime (So I thought). I asked the Lord, "Why would you put me here?" But instead of giving me an answer to my question, He just told me to work hard and be an example. This did not go over very well with me.

As I tried to do what the Lord said, I had a bit of a cocky attitude, acting as though I didn't belong there or others who I worked with were not worthy of being around me or even talking to me, but God saw differently.

God had His hands full with me, yet His Hands were on me. The proof of this is that He never left me alone.

After working for about two weeks, after He humbled me through a few failures on the job, letting me know I did not know everything, I finally was down so far in spirit that I was willing to listen.

The Lord took me to the scripture:

Let everyone be subject to the governing authorities except that which God has established.

The authorities that exist have been established by God.

Romans 13:1, NIV

After reading it, He spoke to my spirit, telling me that the authority that I carried through the badge I wore not only represented Him but that He is the very foundation of where all laws were established; in other words, HE MADE THE LAW! He scolded me, "How dare you take my authority and use it for your own selfish pleasure!"

My lame reply was, "Everybody else has done it and some have done worse and gotten away with it!" His reply? "You ain't everybody else. You can't claim Me as your Savior and yet disobey Me." Then this scripture came to mind, and I knew it was only God.

Whom I love I chastise, because

the Lord disciplines the one He loves.

Hebrews 12:6, NIV

He also told me, "I will fix it so that you will not be able to hire a lawyer to get you off. You will endure the chastisement, learn, and let me build your character to where your life will not be the same. Through this, you will never make that mistake ever again. You will be a better person, pastor, father, and officer. You will carry my badge with the understanding that all authority comes from Me; not the governor, not the Sheriff, not the Chief of police, and not from yourself, but from Me!"

God said "When you were called out to certain calls because of certain disturbances, no matter how dangerous they were, people would stop what they were doing when you arrived, and you were able to take control. It wasn't because people were afraid of you, nor was it because you had control.

Do you remember when Israel went to war? The Ark of the Covenant was carried on the shoulders of the Levite priests and was covered by a black covering that stood for the presence of the Lord. The Levite priests went into battle first with the army following them. The army was always victorious because God was there before them.

As God continued to speak to me, he stated it's the same when you went out to a call. The reason why things fell into place is that through the Holy Spirit, I was there when you arrived. In other words, I fought that battle before you got there.

I was the one who weakened the enemy. *I am the Lord of all. In short, it was Me, not you."* After God was done speaking to me and I finally grasped what He was instilling in me, I learned that having others obey authority is one thing, but knowing who is really in authority is something else entirely. I had to learn to respect the fact that all authority starts with God. Every victory I have, I am very careful to remember to acknowledge God because He is my stronghold during times of confusion or chaos, He is my rock in a weary land, He's my bread when I'm hungry, and my water when I'm thirsty. He is my everything.

The Lord saw fit to restore my badge, and His authority came back to me. However, there is not a day that goes by that I don't acknowledge that He is behind the badge I wear.

In the year of 1988, I attended The East Texas Police Academy. I remember the instructors would always tell us.

"The badge can open many doors, and give you many privileges. People will admire you; some women may fall all over you. But remember, if the badge is taken for granted or used for selfish purposes, the actions while wearing the badge could get you into a lot of trouble."

As a person of color, I didn't fully understand the importance and weight of responsibility in authority until I became a peace officer myself. No matter my color or background, I now realize the gravity of the role and the impact it has on people's lives. That old song we used to sing while I was growing up in church did not mean very much to me; however, I loved singing it. Today it brings so much joy to me because as I'm writing this, I can't hold back my tears.

THE SONG IS,

"**Amazing Grace**"

Amazing grace how sweet the sound
That saved a wretch like me.

I once was lost but now I'm Found.
Was blind but now I see.

John Newton

CHAPTER 2

When Leaders Change the Rules, God Overrules

I once heard a pastor state that,

We have no room for spiritual wimps.

Pastor Ralph Caraway Sr.

In other words, some people want all the rewards of being a Christian yet do all they can to avoid the responsibilities and sacrifices. If we expect to have Christ in our lives, we must have Him during our bad days as well as our good.

Living as Christians is not always a bed of roses. It's no secret that, as Christians, we are more than people who just go to church, shout, sing, or participate in works of the church. We are role models for the world. We are the salt of the earth. The world needs to see how Christians react, especially during the times of crisis. Why?

Christ uses us to introduce Himself to the world through different areas of our lives, whether family members, work, around other friends, get togethers and even churches. Christ wants us to let our light shine that men may see our good works so that He can be glorified; Thus, showing that this is our sole purpose, winning souls to Christ.

These actions show that we are conquerors, even during the worst of times. It shows others what Christ can and will do for those who trust Him.

When looking at the story of Daniel, what comes to mind is how he was thrown into the lion's den for not bowing to a god that was built in the king's image by his servants. This was simply to sleight Daniel considering the king's favor for him. Then God comes and delivers.

Looking deeper into this story, it's more than just being delivered. It's about building character within Daniel. It's about showing leaders and a pagan country, Persia, who God is, that He is in control of the law, and that He is the ultimate authority.

King Darius, who was king at the time and the authority figure, saw nothing but good in Daniel, who was one of the three top governors. The Lord blessed Daniel in this pagan nation because Daniel still remembered the Lord, and gave honor, praises, and respect to Him by praying three times daily.

> **Do not conform any longer to the pattern**
> **of this world but be transformed by**
> **the renewing of your mind.**
>
> **Romans 12:2, NIV**

Just because he was in a pagan nation, this did not change who he was in the Lord.

Keep in mind that no matter how bad the atmosphere among others, or no matter our environment, we don't have to be the product of it. If we are walking in Christ, no matter the situation, it should not change who we are in Him. God still blesses and keeps us if we remain

Daniel is a wonderful example of this. Daniel knew his strength, blessing, and his sense of being came from the Lord. Daniel understood that God has control over all things, so much so that he knew evil could not do anything without God's permission.

Whether it be leaders or kings, good or wicked, God is in control. The Bible tells us:

In the Lord's hand the King's heart is a stream of water that He channels toward all who please Him.

Proverbs 21:1, NIV

If we look at the history of Daniel's life, at the age of 15 or 16, he, along with Azariah, Mishael, Hananiah (known as Shadrach, Meshach, and Abednego) the nation of Judah was captured by Babylon. Along with Daniel, all three of these Hebrew boys were placed in the palace to serve King Nebuchadnezzar.

Through the testing of foods, interpreting of dreams, and handwriting on the wall, witnessing the challenge of the three Hebrew boys placed in the fiery furnace and delivered by God Himself, and later with Babylon being attacked by Persia and now under a new king, Darius, Daniel continued to grow in the Lord and trust Him for all his needs.

Now at the age of about 80, Daniel was more likely to be even closer to God than he had ever been.

With his character displaying such quality, he was noticed by the new King Darius.

So pleased with Daniel, the king wanted to promote him to head governor above all others, second command only to himself. Keep in mind that Daniel was a Hebrew and Hebrews were looked down upon as slaves by Babylon who had been concurred by Persia and lived under their empire.

When the other governors, who were Babylonians, heard about King Darius wanting to promote Daniel, (I'm sure because Daniel was always viewed as a slave by Babylon), they probably thought to themselves, "You will not promote that Hebrew slave over us." The first thing they tried to do was find fault in Daniel's work and character. Keep in mind, when God is about to use us to introduce Himself, the enemy starts his attacks.

When they could not find anything against Daniel, even in his personal life, they chose to tamper with the only thing that could affect him: his relationship with God.

Knowing that Daniel was one of the chief administrators, had favor with the king, the leaders, along with all other administrators, decided to meet with the King without Daniel for the sheer purpose of pulling off a scheme. Let me take a brief pause and say this. Some of us feel that just because we are a minority, society will look down on us, not promote us, or find some way to keep us under its thumb to control us in the way it wants us to go.

Although this may be the intent for some, Daniel is a prime example that if God wants us to have something, whether blessings, promotions, or even favor with others, no one on this earth can stop us from receiving it if we live in His will. However, if we give it up or react in such a way that our testimony would be in question, we could forfeit our blessings.

We say we believe in God, and we trust Him; yet, we rebel against His authority. Or, as soon as our faith is tested, our reaction causes bad behavior, such as disrespecting or lashing out at others because of our problems. We con, swindle, or put down others to lift up ourselves; then we try to cover it up with some religious rhetoric.

As Christians, when we see certain authorities in power change rules, break laws, or deceive others for their purposes, we should not react in a way to imitate them or seek vengeance. The Bible says,

Vengeance is mine saith the Lord, I will repay.

Romans 12:19, NIV

Some may feel that we deserve to react how we want because we have been wronged and, by any means necessary, need to be vindicated. With this type of attitude, we are doing right in our own eyes and falling into the trap of the enemy. Everyone has the right to be vindicated; however, it depends on how we vindicate. It does not give us the right to do wrong.

In the movie Glory, there was a scene where Morgan Freeman (Sgt Rollins) slapped Denzel Washington (Tripp) because he (Tripp) felt that he was treated unfairly by the system. So, he decided that he wanted to take his frustration out on one of his fellow soldiers. Rollins said, *"So you have been whipped and chased by hounds. It ain't living and it's sure as hell ain't dying"*. In other words, things happen in life and it could have been the worst experience that we have had. However, how we handle our experiences will determine how our character will shape in life.

We can allow ourselves to become bitter, taking our frustrations out on others by lashing out at them. We can have our characters shaped in such a way that we will always fly off the handle if things don't work out to our expectations. Or we can live in denial and act as though our problem does not exist, only to have it come up later in life, destroying new personal relationships, working relationships, or organizational relationships. Or, like Daniel, we can choose to give it to God and continue to worship Him, praising Him through our problems while He is working them out.

King Darius, who was trying to unify a nation after the defeat of Babylon, (which is normal for new leaders) was extremely excited when all the chief administrators, leaders, and all other governors met with him to sign a decree into law which stated, that no one could bow to any god but Darius for 30 days. Of course, Daniel was not invited to this meeting because they changed the rules for him.

The King, who was full of himself, proud of the people who were coming together, and not having a clue what they were doing, did not hesitate to sign the decree, thinking this would unify the nation and receive praise from all the people in the land. His signing made it an order to where it could not be altered or retracted.

Daniel, again, who served and believed in the true living God, heard the news but continued to bow down to the Lord three times a day as he always did with his windows wide open. Daniel never had anything to hide. His life was always an open book, not only for the people he worked for, but also for his own people, Israel, to where he could be a continual example for his faith in the Lord. Things were about to change for Daniel.

He was about to be blind-sided, or so the others thought. He was about to face one of the biggest challenges in his career and in his life. Daniel was up for the challenge.

It's so amazing that when we are walking with God, just when things are beginning to look up, or blessings are about to come, the enemy has a way of trying to block the blessings, putting our testimony in question, or damaging who we are in the Lord.

Whether a promotion, raise, children doing well, a beautiful relationship, or even just your character, the enemy will have something to say, crude remarks to hurt you. Even if you have done nothing wrong, the enemy will try to dig up dirt on you simply to accuse you of something you did not do. Even when we make a mistake, he (the enemy) exaggerates the incident to frustrate us.

However, there is a flip side to this. God uses these setbacks to strengthen our faith in Him, to show us where we are in our faith, or simply to prepare our character for a bigger blessing ahead.

How we handle these setbacks will be totally up to us. We can whine, cry and complain about our circumstances, blaming others for our mishaps; or, we can use those same circumstances, cry to God, and wait for Him in His own time to deliver.

Those of us, who have a history with God, know that He will not let challenges take us so far and leave us.

God always has a plan and that is to grow and make us better than we were the day before. Therefore, I learned to praise God through my circumstances because if He has delivered before, I know without a shadow of a doubt that He will do it again.

When God delivers....... look out!

BECAUSE HE WILL DO it. The Bible says,

But those who hope in the Lord will renew their strength. They will soar on wings like eagles; they will run and not grow weary, they will walk and not be faint.

Isaiah 40:31, NIV

If we just wait on the Lord, we will have the opportunity to witness Him as He shows up and shows out.

If we just wait on the Lord, we will see our enemies fall or disarm right before us. If we wait on the Lord, we will see hearts soften, doors open, crooked roads straighten, and wasteland become an oasis.... Wait for Him!

The Bible clearly states

Whoever is ashamed of me and my words,

the Son of Man will be ashamed of them when He comes in His glory and in all glory of the Father and of the holy angels.

Luke 9:26, NIV

If we have a relationship with Christ as we say, our lives should reflect that character. Ups and downs in life are inevitable. There's no way of getting around it; however, through Christ, we are victors. Therefore, our lives should be an open book, not only for us so that people can see God move in our lives, but also to inspire others to grow in the Lord Jesus Christ and to seek His face in the time of trouble.

When the leaders found Daniel, they caught him praying to his God about them. Daniel could have held a protest, could have tried to argue them down, or could have gotten others to side with him and held a rebellion, but he chose to tell God about it.

There are days when we try to do the best we can to serve God. There are those who become jealous of our blessings and sometimes even our character. They wonder how we can stay so upbeat amid problems and persevere.

At times, some try to step on us, mistreat us, or speak all manner of things about us to others, attempting to destroy us as a person, yet we still flourish. We bloom where we are planted.

No matter how dark the days are, or how dark people try to make your circumstances, we have a light that cannot be hidden. We don't hide behind a bushel of hatred, deception, mudslinging, or backbiting. Why is this? Because we know we have a problem solver, a burden bearer. We know we have the rock of Gibraltar an anchor amid a storm.

**You prepare a table before me in
the presence of my enemies.**

23rd **Psalms, NIV**

The more the devil tempts us and tries to keep us down or when others try to knock us down, or when life lets us down, the more the Lord will bless and lift us up in the presence of our enemies.

Although we are not perfect, and on occasions we fall, we know who to go to when we fall, slip, or lose our way. We go to the only one who can fix our situation and gives us strength during our weakest times. His Name... Jesus. Do you remember when Peter walked on the water? If he kept his eyes on Jesus, he was afloat. As soon as he was distracted by the storms around him, he began to sink.

What I loved about Peter was when he was sinking, he Called Jesus to help him. Jesus reached down to pick him up. Peter knew who to call on when he was sinking. In the times of our failures, troubles, heartaches, pains, and when we are sinking in despair, all we must do is call on His name and He will save us.

After seeing Daniel praying to the Lord our God, they thought they really had him.

They could not wait to get to King Darius to tell him all that Daniel was doing. Of course, when they enthusiastically told the king, the king was not happy about it. In fact, the king did all he could to clear Daniel, but it was no use. The petition became a law when he signed it. Hear me right. It was the Law.

King Darius summoned Daniel to come before him. After giving him every opportunity to bow down to him, Daniel still refused. But keep in mind he never rebelled against the Authority nor the leader. We can disagree with the system when they are breaking the laws of God, but it gives us no right to break the law with harmful retaliation. For example, there is a story about Robin Hood, who allegedly stole from the rich to give to the poor. Stealing is stealing. It's a crime, no matter who it is. It doesn't stop being a sin because a person had done us some kind of harm. Remember what the word says?

**Vengeance is mine saith the
Lord, I will repay!**

Romans 12:19, NIV

Did you think this was written for the sake of just being written? No! It was written to let us know that God is in charge, and He is in control. Without any resistance, Daniel was placed in the lion's den. The king sealed the den with his signet ring to show no favoritism toward Daniel in any way. Daniel did not know how or in what manner God was going to deliver him, but based on his history with God, he knew He was going to do something. He also knew that God had been too good to him to give in, placing another god before Him.

Therefore, in the end, Daniels's faith in God paid off. Just when his accusers thought they had him, had gotten rid of him, and had destroyed him, God saw differently. He sent an angel to that very den to comfort Daniel as the lions surrounded him. All that night, not one touched him.

During this time, King Darius was so worried about Daniel that he could not sleep. Early that morning, he went to the lion's den and called out to Daniel in a voice of anguish, *"Did your God deliver you?"*

Daniel answered, "Yes, oh King, because I was innocent toward God and you." Daniel remained blameless, even when his accusers continued to trap him. He remained blameless during his darkest days. Not only did God deliver, but his accusers ended up suffering the same fate that was placed on him, the lion's den.

What others tried to stop Daniel from getting, it came. When those leaders tried to change the rules in their favor, God overruled them. This proves again that if God wants us to have something, nothing can stop us from getting it unless we give up or forfeit through sinful reactions or retaliation.

When the world was in a sin debt, it could only be paid by blood. The devil thought he could have the world do what he pleased, but it was someone who came that he did not expect, Jesus.

When he came into the world, the devil tried to destroy everything Jesus was building while on the earth. The devil thought he had Him. Thought he beat Him. When they put Him in a borrowed tomb, the enemy thought there was no way out.

The tomb was sealed by the Chief Priest, the Pharisees with the help of Pontius Pilate thinking that was it for Jesus. He's done. I can hear the enemy asking, *"Death do you have Him?" Death said, "Yes, I have Him." "Sin, do you have Him?" Sin said, "Yes, we have Him." "Grave do you have Him?" Grave replied, "Yes, we have Him. He's not going anywhere."*

What the enemy didn't know is that even when he had the law put Jesus on the cross and in the tomb, just as Daniel was lifted out of the dungeon through the grace of King Darius, it was the grace and love of God that got Jesus out on the third day. It was a new day. A glorious day. A victorious day. A day the devil never thought could happen.

The Bible tells us

God so loved the world that He gave His only begotten Son, that whoever believes in him shall not perish but have eternal life

John 3:16, NIV

The law is meant to govern the actions of this world, but the law does not save. Jesus does. The laws cannot change the hearts of men. Jesus can. The law itself does not show compassion, but Jesus is full of compassion.

CHAPTER 3

Where Do We Go From Here?

As Americans, we live in one of the most blessed places in the world. God has been so good to us in this country that one can't imagine the countless blessings we receive just waking up in the morning. However, I have some theological questions about us as Christians in America. Whether black, white, poor, rich, Methodist, Baptist, or Pentecostal, we all live in this country together.

My question would be why we hate one another so much. What is it about us that keeps us separated from one another? Especially Christian people who supposedly know Christ on a personal level.

We sing those beautiful Christian songs of loving the Lord and others, working together to improve the world.

Yet our attitudes reflect something different and as much as I hate to admit, this also includes me.

Yes, me! I am just as guilty as everyone else because there are many days, I may not have participated in some of the wrongdoings, but like many of us, I did nothing to at least try to correct it. In my mind it wasn't my business, why rock the boat? If I'm getting mine and the Lord is taking care of me and mine, why worry about others? When I came to my senses it suddenly hit me, I found how lost I was.

We as Christian people allow the things of this world to separate us from Christ and the evidence of that is how we treat one another. We let politics take over our lives to the point where Christ is used only when He is convenient for us.

The Bible tells us, let your light so shine that men may see your good works and glorify your Father in heaven. Many of us speak of Christ but what are our intentions? Many of us do the works of the Lord if there is something in it for us, such as power, money, prestige, respect, etc.

Politics plays an important role in our walk with Jesus or lack thereof. For example, every morning I would wake up around 5:00 am. The first thing I do is turn on the television and watch the news. Parts of me have excitement in my spirit because my political party looks as though it's coming back! (Not affiliated with any party today) Some mornings, I watch the news, and the other party seems to be getting ahead.

I am then very disappointed and disturbed because, in my heart, I want to feel that my party is on the right track, doing all the right things, and making all the right moves. I wanted to be sure they were serving the Lord the way they are supposed to, "My Way". It doesn't matter who we (My party) put in office if those politicians fight for my agenda or if I have who I like in office. No matter the outrageous decision they make, I'm ok with them. If others have a problem with them, my attitude is TOUGH!

We won, get over it, and you better accept them, because that person is good for all of us, unlike the one you all (The other party) tried to vote in. You all know the one we voted in is good for this country. I don't see why you all don't see it my way.

You need to follow me and the one I voted for because I follow Christ!

When I saw that other parties, organizations, and social clubs were reacting the same as I was, but for the opposite of what I believed, I was offended.

How dare you! (Trying to reason with myself, I thought.) Of course, people have a right to their opinions, but (In my mind) I'm right. Why don't people see that? Everyone has the right to their thoughts if they follow my guidelines.

Unfortunately, here in America, our God-fearing nation, we can admit it or not, most of us think like this. This attitude has also filtered into the evangelical community causing hatred, prejudices, and just total bad behavior. The Bible tells us in Colossians 3:2 (NIV) "Set your minds on things above, not on earthly things."

It is really disturbing when Christians adopt the attitude of the world in our actions, and then justify it through Christ and His word!

No matter the color, culture, background, or political affiliation, this does not excuse bad behavior or how we treat our fellow man. This leads to some of us thinking of only ourselves and what we believe.

These days and times, the love of God has waxed cold. Lack of respect runs rampant among one another. We try to justify our arguments by some political party or group and its rhetoric and again, trying to include Jesus during it all and again making selfish statements such as, "Follow me because I follow Christ" when the statement should say, as Paul says, "Follow me as I follow Christ"!

None of us have a monopoly on all the truth. We are all trying to find our way, growing and learning in Christ. In this growth, there should be encouragement and lifting one another.

This is not to say we will not have our disagreement, which will happen, but if we are one with Christ like most of us want to believe, then we should have a desire to reconcile with one another.

Accept one another differences, and at times agree to disagree and continue to do the works of Christ. For example, in Acts 15:36-39 Paul and Barnabas were in a heated argument because Barnabas wanted John Mark to accompany them to check on those cities where they preached the word. Paul sharply said no because John Mark abandoned them in the past. Although they were in a heated disagreement, both knew they had one goal in mind, spreading the Gospel.

Their disagreement did not stop the work of Christ. They agreed to disagree and split up. Paul took Silas and Barnabas took John Mark.

They later reconciled and their relationship grew stronger. Unfortunately, reconciliation is not happening today in the body of Christ, the Church. My question is, where do we go from here?

With all the war of words, the panic, the hurts, and pains that we cause toward one another with all the unnecessary words (Tough talk) used to win arguments at any cost. Where do we go from here?

When it comes to Jesus, there are no big I's and little you's. In His eyes, we are all His children, and we are all as one. However, greed for power and the love of money have overtaken us as Christian people to a whole new level of hatred. Satan is having a field day with American Christians. What's sad is, that it's not just leaders tearing us as Christian Americans apart, we as Christians choose to be torn apart.

We forget about forgiveness and reconciliation. If some of us choose to reconcile, we will only forgive on our terms or at times, not at all, while giving fake smiles or smooth agreeable gestures, while plotting to harm or hurt one another.

In these perilous times, however, some of us again, wear the label as Christian, but our actions show something different, which makes some of us in total denial of our actions. It's like a drug addiction, we feel as though we don't have a problem, but everyone else does, and the truth could be glaring in our faces.

If we are Christians like we say we are, then we need to be strong enough to be brutally honest with ourselves to recognize our problems or shortcomings, make a change in our lives for the better, stand up for what is right in the eyes of God and not lean to our understanding.

The Bible tells us in the book of Joshua 2:7 (NIV) The people served the Lord throughout the lifetime of Joshua and the Elders who outlived him and who had seen all the great things the Lord had done for Israel.

I am a firm believer that Christians who are 75 or 80 and above are the last of the prayer warriors of our time. We need to embrace them and get as much knowledge as we can while they are living. These Christians knew what it was like to fight and pray, not that they were perfect because none of us are, but they had something to fight for; they had something to pray for.

There were challenges back in the day, such as wars, WW1, WW2, the Korean War, and the Vietnam War etc. And as hard as for this to believe, blacks and other races not only fought in these wars, but they also had a burning desire to fight for our country, not feeling that no one owed them anything in return.

Even when we were separated by race, God had a way of placing us together to where we had to depend on one another and come together for a common cause.

In other words, looking over color or culture, we had no choice but to fight side by side. This is how some of us brutally found out that we were all one in Christ and that we needed one another. These challenges affected our way of living to where civilians were participating in trying to do their part such as donations of not only monies, but scrap metal, aluminum, volunteer work, entertainment for troops, etc. Many seem to be doing so much that they have no time for nonsense or fighting over petty issues. They had bigger eggs to fry.

Let's not forget, during those times there was also, Jim Crowism, voter's rights, Women's rights, and equal rights, and as hard as for some to believe, there were some Whites, Mexicans, and even other races who fought, prayed and marched with people of color.

Some of them, if not most, lost the support of their own families, were put out of their homes by family members, became victims of violent behaviors of their counterparts, lost friendships, jobs, and some even their lives for the sake of doing what was right in God's eyes. However, even during these perilous times, most actually saw God move in their circumstances, and some even in their lives.

With most, God was taken seriously, so seriously that it was acknowledged through their presence in church service and worship. God help us if we missed church, we would not feel right, and our day would not be fulfilled until we went to church.

We had a serious prayer meeting because we had something to pray for.

We had something to fight for. As hard as life had been, life had purpose and meaning and because of that, God meant something in our lives.

Worship service was moving, to the point we felt the presence of God. We would sing the song "Yes God is real" because He was real in our souls. We saw God move, we saw Him soften hearts, open doors that we never would think would be open, and even to the so-called worst of people later in the years, turn their lives around and start running for Jesus as Paul did in the book of Acts when Christ changed his life for good while on the road to Damascus.

The question I would ask all of us Christians is, where do we go from here? It also says in Joshua 17:6 (NIV) that in those days Israel had no king; everyone did as they saw fit. Or (What was right in their minds). This led to so much political corruption and God's people fighting with one another.

The Corinthian Church Christians, however, had the same problem as Christians today. They were extremely corrupt, and Paul had to send a letter of reprimand to them, not once, but twice. Most of them respected Paul, but there was a minority who would speak against Paul and allowed certain preachers, who were great orators, who presented great, compelling arguments and would not sacrifice anything or suffer one bit as Paul did in the furtherance of the gospel.

Instead, they lead many away from the true gospel of Jesus Christ. Anything that sounds good, feels good or looks good, these Christians would fall for as Christian Americans are falling for this today. The evidence is proof of the decay of America. The hatred, back-biting, and deception. The Bible tells us in Matthew 5:13, we are the salt of the Earth. What does salt do?

Salt preserves and keeps. It also brings out the flavor in food to make it tasty and delightful to eat. If we are Christians, as the salt of the earth, we bring out the best in people as salt brings out the best in food. When people see a Christian, because they see Christ in us, it should bring out the best in others to the point that they want to do what is right, not by our standards but by God's.

However, there is also a flip side to this; when salt is poured into an open wound, it burns.

At times everyone will not like us. Especially if we are making attempts to do what is right in the eyes of God. Some, when they see us, just our presence will upset them, realizing they are not living in Christ themselves. There are times when we may have to stand for what is right in Christ or make unpopular decisions that go against the world's liking.

This makes some upset, not only for the stand, but it's a reminder that they are to live for Christ, and it also can bring them to shame, especially those Christians who step out of Character or purpose and lose sight of Christ.

Salt also makes us thirsty, As Christians, when people see us, our ways, actions, and speech ought to make them thirsty for Christ! When others have tried everything else for any kind of spiritual relief, they should be able to look at a Christian and the Christian should make them want to know Christ.

When Christians lose this characteristic (Drawing Power), then they have blended in with the world, they have lost their power to season the world. As the bible says, salt has lost its saltiness. This creates misunderstandings, jumping to conclusions, hatred of righteousness for one another, pride, haughtiness, lying, and perversion of every kind. In saying this, this is not to say we participate in it but we now turn our heads when it happens, which makes us just as guilty.

The Bible tells us in 1st Peter 5:8-9(NIV) to be alert and sober mind. Your enemy the devil prowls around like a roaring lion, looking for someone to devour. Resist him, standing firm in the faith because you know that the family of believers throughout the world is undergoing the same kind of suffering.

These days and times, we do not want to face reality about ourselves. Many of us will believe a beautiful lie of some American dream than face the harsh truth of reality that we have left the Lord! We are slowly becoming our own worst enemy. What better way to tear something apart than having it work against itself? America doesn't have to worry about war when we have it within ourselves.

And if we don't wake up, while we are warring within ourselves, another country can and probably will come and overtake us as Babylon overtook Israel back in the biblical days when they became drunk among themselves and drunk physically. The same with Babylon when Persia attacked them. They felt that they were invincible. They could not be touched or overtaken! But God saw otherwise.

People may or may not agree with me on this, but I had a huge wake-up call within myself on this issue. Because change starts with the individual, it may as well start with me. I had to face some painful realities about myself. Again, I just happened to be reading the book of Judges one day and the first chapter hit me like a ton of bricks. This is when Joshua and the elders

(Who always put God first in all things) died and people started thinking they were right in their minds.

Because of my selfish thoughts, this convinced me in my spirit to start looking at myself instead of criticizing others. As I questioned myself, I asked, "Am I thinking what is right in my mind? Is all of this about God or me?" I felt like Saul, who was smitten by the light of the truth.

I tried to justify my beliefs with an argument that America is a racist country where the rich care about only themselves, therefore, I must look out for number one. Me! After all, no one else is going to do it. But then something hit me and that was, "But God" He is in charge.

Continuing to reason with myself, I went on to think, "Don't get me wrong, I believe in God, but God wants me to look out for myself. It's not selfishness, it common sense! If everyone would look out for themselves, you know? Pull themselves up by there on bootstraps, America would be a better place.

If whites don't like it, they go back to Iceland, Europe, Italy, Scotland, Ireland, Great Britain, Germany, Australia, or wherever their race comes from. Blacks can go back to Africa, Spanish can go back to Spain, Mexicans can go back to Mexico where they belong, and Muslims, go back to the Middle East. I guess Israel can come or go as they please because you know if we don't take care of them, God will probably blow us to kingdom come or we will not have this prosperity that we are having now." Then a thought came to my head again.... "But God"

As I began to grow in the Lord, questions about salvation and Christianity started plaguing my mind. I started feeling miserable, I felt like my life was out of control or I was losing control. But then the thought again came to my head. "But God" As I began to try to figure out these feelings I was having, Isaiah 6 came to mind. It spoke of how Isaiah saw the purity of God with all his glory and realized that he had to make a change in his life. He began to realize that the people whom he did not like because of their sins, he was one of them. He lived among them for so long that he began to adopt their ways.

He was such a part of them that he did not see his wrongs. When he finally saw himself as he was. He felt shame, hurt; a little lost, and overtaken about who he was and what he had become. What I loved about Isaiah was he didn't just see who he was, he took steps to change. One was being brutally honest with himself, which is hard to do, and the other was that he made a change for the good. When he made his change, his attitude also changed. Instead of hurting others, he wanted others to change to have a relationship with God so that they could stop hurting themselves.

Unfortunately, they were so one-sided and deep in their sins that they felt no need to change.

When I look at the political parties and organizations, not some, but every one of them, it disturbs me about our actions toward one another. Let me make something clear, back in the day, we all had differences of opinion.

We will have that if we are on this earth, but we have respect for one another and work things out. We understood this was the Christian thing to do. It doesn't mean that we compromised our Christianity.

Today, it's as though America is like a ship with all of us together; political parties, cultures, races, and a storm could come and overtake us. There is panic everywhere. No one is listening to one another, no one is communicating. Everyone is telling one another you don't belong on the boat; others are rocking the boat trying to get in but remember, a storm is in effect, and everyone is working against one another. Soon the ship will crash, not because we could not keep it together, but because we refused to work together.

Again, Joshua 2:7 says the people serve the Lord throughout the timeline of Joshua and of the elders who outlived him and who had seen all the great things the Lord has done for Israel. The problem is, our generation today because we have no struggles and we are living off the blessings of our forefathers from the past, we can't see and probably will not ever see God move. Although we go to church, sing glorious songs, and wave holy hands, deep down, we feel we do not need God. Prosperity, oppression, sexual offenses along with immoral behavior are the norm. Christians consistently hide their light behind a bushel due to political parties and pressures of others who deceive many to fatten their own pockets with more wealth and political muscle.

Many of them say we are here to create more jobs, and some do it for the good of society, others create jobs only to play with others' lives like a chess game, confusing to sway society in their favor or to get what they want. My question again is, where do we go from here?

Do we continue to ride this ship, fighting among one another? Right now, the sun is shining, the weather is presentable. We had storms from time to time that we have weathered. My question is what we are going to do when a real storm comes?

In the book of Acts 27th chapter, Paul was on a ship as a prisoner. He warned the ship workers not to make a certain voyage because the time of the season was not presentable for sailing due to storms and high winds. The captain and the owner chose not to listen to Paul, making the voyage. Soon a storm came battered against the ship.

The storm was so bad that even the experienced sailors were trying to sneak off the ship until Paul caught and confronted them. Although they were afraid for their lives, they all had no choice but to work together and stay on the ship. The ship ended up destroyed by the storm crashing into the rocks, but they all lived floating on shore on broken pieces.

America is not in a storm right now, but the decisions leaders are making for their politically selfish views can cost us and get us into such a white-knuckling storm that we can lose this old ship of Zion that we call America. I don't know about you, but I'd rather not be forced to work with others because of desperate circumstances.

I will not want to be forced to love someone for just survival purposes or to just get along, I want to work with others because of the love of Christ in me.

None of us have all the answers, but I believe through my research, I pray that I can at least arouse others' interest to the point where they would at least explore why serving the Lord will pay off if we seek peace through Him, not our way but Gods way.

CHAPTER 4

America and People of Color

The more my relationship with God deepens along with the reading of His word, the more I am convinced that America was established to be the melting pot for the spread of the Gospel of Christ all over the world. Though not perfect, with all its flaws and deep-hearted racism, this did not stop the gospel from spreading, it enhanced it even more. When people are being oppressed in any way, they may become very rebellious and undisciplined, becoming the very people who oppressed them and start oppressing one another.

Others may endure it with the hope of just getting by or surviving yet become so bitter with their lives that they become stagnate to where they have no goals, hopes, or dreams. They are so busy reliving the times of oppression that they can't move on. It's one thing to remember where we came from and build from it.

It's something else when we get so angry that we do nothing; and still with others, it enhances spirituality. It causes them to search for some purpose or reason why and what they must do to end oppression.

For people of color, most of us found Christ. Although those who sought power or sought to keep it by using Christ and His word to justify slavery, violent attacks on the weak, and fattening their pockets with profits from the backs of slavery, the truth in the gospel still prevailed.

God still moved and moved in powerful ways, especially through people of color. I'm reminded of the story of a man whom God asked to push a huge rock.

Not understanding what God was up to, he placed total trust in God and began to push the rock. Days, months and soon a couple of years had gone by. Noticing that the rock only moved an inch, he began to inquire of God about this situation.

He stated,

> Lord, I did what you asked, and two years have gone by with only the rock moving an inch, forgive me Lord, but I feel I'm not accomplishing very much I feel that this is a waste of time." The Lord answered him most wonderfully and replied. I'm sorry you feel this way, but there is a purpose for everything I do.

Author Unknown

The Lord continued and said,

> Now, stand straight up and look at yourself, your shoulders have become broader, your chest, arms, and legs have gotten bigger and stronger, and your wind has improved! I did not tell you to push the rock for the rock to move, I told you to push the rock for you to grow!

Author Unknown

As we cried, whaled, and petitioned God amid oppression; not knowing what the future held, we praised God regardless. Though our situation did not change right away, our relationship with Christ grew so much that not only did our hearts grow deeper in Him, it caused our relationship to grow even stronger. As our gifts and talents developed, it enhanced our wit and cleverness. Not only did we learn to think quickly on our feet more quickly than others, but we also learned endurance and survival skills through horrifically difficult times.

As a result of witnessing the horrendous experiences people of color endured, inspired the onlookers to serve God with steadfastness. Most of all, at least not that I know of, I don't know any race of people who love God like we do. In short, "We love us some God!" Granted we have our moments of disobedience, and we fall short. But we still honor Christ even now.

Do you remember the story of Joseph in Genesis, Chapters 37 through 45 when he was thrown in a pit by his brothers, then later sold into slavery? Unbeknownst to what the future held for him; Joseph became a slave under a man by the name of Potiphar in the land of Egypt. He soon won the full trust of Potiphar to where he was running the affairs of the whole house. Just as things were about to look up for him, Potipher's wife started making advances toward him.

Due to him resisting her advances, out of frustration and spite, she accused Joseph of making advances toward her and he was placed in prison.

As unfair as this was, Joseph still held on to his faith in the Lord. His positive spiritual character led him to become Head Trustee. No matter how dark his days were, his light shined even brighter. Despite his situation, he bloomed where he was planted.

That same spiritual character moved him to interpret a dream for the Baker who ended up executed and the Butler who ended up restored to his position. He asked the Butler to remember him when he went before the King, however, the Butler forgot all about Joseph. As a result, he spent two more years in prison yet still served the Lord. When the king needed a dream interpreted and found no one in the land to do it, the Butler recommended Joseph.

The king summoned Joseph, he interpreted the dream, and quickly rose in the ranks as governor of Egypt, 2nd only to the pharaoh. This took about 17 years of the most tumultuous hardships of his life for God to prepare him for this position. Keep in mind that Joseph was a Hebrew, and they were looked down upon by Egyptians, yet look how God works. God promotes who He wants when He wants, how He wants, and for His purpose.

This proves, that if God wants to bless us or promote us, no matter our background, our race, gender, or culture no one can stop it.

However, we must be willing to always trust Him, not when the feeling suits us or when days are good.

We must trust Him through the good days as well as the bad. Sylvester Stallone said it best in the movie Rocky Balboa

> **It's about how hard you get hit and keep moving forward, how much you can take and keep moving forward.**
>
> **Sylvester Stallone**

But let me add this twist, we have God every step of the way, and are never left alone.

God will use challenging circumstances to shape our character and to prepare us not only for breakthrough blessings but for bigger challenges ahead. Though Christ was beaten into us through slavery, He also revealed His true self for us and through us. We have seen God move in the most extraordinary ways during the most difficult times. We've seen the most difficult doors open, the coldest hearts soften, we have seen barriers torn down and ways made out of no ways.

This by any means does not imply that God has ever condoned slavery; HE DID NOT! nor did He ever.

As God's creation, He gave us free will, and some of us misused our free will and His grace to oppress others. However, those who have been victimized in any way, if they trusted God, were victorious no matter what state they were in as well as taken to higher heights spiritually. God has used them to do extraordinary works for His glory.

We Have Spiritual Power

If we, as people of color, only knew the spiritual power that we have, we could see where God has brought us and appreciate how far we have come. It was God that freed us from slavery and molded us through the fiery trials of segregation and Jim Crowism. Our characters were shaped in such a way that not only were we the spiritual bedrock in building America, but we were also used by God to shape and inspire America.

No other race, except for the Jews, did not endure what we have endured and flourished as we have. not only were inventions made by us, but laws were also passed because of us. There was a time when we could not cross the tracks into a clean, nonracial society. Today, because of the sacrifice of our forefathers, though not perfect, we have been blessed to not only cross the tracks into a society that will accept us but also allow us to flourish and reach for the stars with little opposition.

With God, we have come a long way, but there is still much work to be done. The enemy (Satan) still wants to keep us in certain places where we can't flourish. Our forefathers have endured, suffered and some lost their lives working, enduring, and praying toward a tomorrow that they could have only dreamed about, yet we are now living today.

I can't imagine how hard it was to live back then, constantly praying, praising, and depending on the Lord with the many challenges they had to conquer.

It seems when one challenge has been overcome, several others would spring up, which I'm sure was not only discouraging but also overwhelming. For example, many of us had businesses back in those challenging days.

We had to endure the unfairness of legal procedures, unfair taxes or interest on loans that were so high that we could barely make it, yet we were so determined, even in those days, to reach for the stars.

Some of us suffered from losing property, land, or businesses with contracts so levied, that if we were late or missed one payment, we could lose everything.

We suffered with buildings being burned or bombed, property damaged and at times harassed or lynched on that very same property. In addition, there are many of our white and Hispanic brothers and sisters as well as brothers and sisters who suffered heavily, they lost family support, friendships, homes, businesses, and their lives due to fighting this war with us.

We cannot forget these brave spiritual soldiers. Thank you and God bless and prosper you. Your families because of our determination, despite opposition, with God, who was at the forefront of our victories and achievements, we were able to build, not only places of worship but also Historically Black Colleges and Universities, Seminaries; businesses such as hair care products, food stores, dry cleaning, gas stations, record companies, contractors, etc.

We developed and used our God-given talents and gifts soaring us to such immeasurable heights that some of us were recognized all over the world!

We were the products of many inventions such as the red light, cotton gin, mobile refrigeration units, cell phones, and ironing boards, just to name a few. We were the first to perform open heart surgery, create blood plasma; find cures for many diseases, etc. As Israel built Egypt through slavery, we practically built America, not only through slavery but also as freedmen.

If someone says we have not contributed to America and claims that we are not patriotic, I'm very adamant in saying this is false. Though accused and labeled as being cowardly, and not too bright, we have proven ourselves to not only be extremely patriotic, but also by fighting in every war for America as well as The Revolutionary War of 1775 and a few other countries. Many victories have been won in our regiments as well as fighting side by side with whites.

I'm reminded of one example of the 761st black Tank Regiment who were called the Black Panthers during World War 2. Though General George Patton had a certain social order and his racial ways, he still acknowledged the courage and bravery of this regiment. Due to the heat of the war, he needed all men.

He proved this by making the statement,

**I don't care what color you are as long as
you go up there and kill those Kraut sons a bi$%!.**

General George Patton

Many were awarded metals of honor, along with purple hearts...

Some have credited people of color for turning the tides of war or concurring territories, yet, in most history books, either we were given very little credit, or many times, not mentioned at all. Many other races and organizations are riding on the skirt tails of laws that were passed because of people of color and at times some act as though they are victimized by the very laws that some have created themselves!

For instance, some laws were passed to keep minorities from voting but when it backfired, then suddenly it became an issue. As people of color, today, some of us are still treated unfairly due to certain laws being passed such as taking history out of schools, gerrymandering in voter's rights, and justifying their actions by policy and even religious rhetoric.

There were accusations of us destroying property through protests or certain marches and accused of being too militant or too forceful when speaking up. We ask ourselves; do we have the right to defend ourselves? Do we have the right to speak up for what is right for everyone? What can we do? What can we do to stand up for ourselves?

Do we have any rights at all? These are great questions, and my answer is absolutely, yes. We have the right to defend ourselves in the Lord.

I repeat, IN THE LORD. However, we need not trust God when it's convenient for us, but trust God as our forefather have; not knowing the future but knowing that He holds the future. Whether good days as well as bad, knowing that He has delivered before, and He will deliver.

Keep in mind that there will always be challenges, some even unfair, especially when it has to do with some kind of change or when confronting a situation where some of us have been violated or when certain leaders or politicians are changing laws.

Or rules to benefit themselves, and again, using the term "Policy" or using Christianity to advocate their cause, and as soon as it backfires, they again, I repeat, "Play the victim." Knowing that this is wrong!

However, today, I must ask us as people of color some hard questions. If I'm too harsh forgive me, with our rights being violated one way or another, yet, while pointing out everyone else's wrong, are we doing right ourselves while confronting these issues?

In saying all this, are we keeping one another in check in doing what is right in the Lord ourselves just as we are expecting others to keep in check? Are we doing right by serving the Lord and trusting Him or are we using Him to hide our sins through church attendance or participation in activities with no intent to change our hearts?

Are we putting too much trust in changing the system according to our standards emulating our oppressors? Don't get me wrong, I love equal rights, but I don't need the equal wrongs to go with it. This is why God must stay in the forefront of our battles because If He is not, the very issues or people we fight against, we can become or emulate.

Watch and pray so that you will not fall into temptation. The spirit is willing but the flesh is weak.

Matthew 26:41, NIV

I see why the bible tells us to watch and pray because it's so easy to lose spiritual focus due to behaviors or lack of responsibilities. And due to the actions of others doing wrong yet seem to get away with it. This can get so difficult that it can become discouraging.

For many years our forefathers just wanted a fair shake and a hand, not a handout.

Although not perfect, we made sure we were doing right by God in our actions, which showed in our characters, despite our oppressors, who were doing wrong and justified it by hiding behind Jesus. Those who have a personal relationship with Him know that Jesus never has or will condone this type of behavior, no matter who we are.

The Bible tells us:

Do not be deceived, God cannot be mocked, A man reaps that he sows.

Galatians 6:7, NIV

Most of us kept ourselves in check to where we would not seek revenge for the sake of getting the upper hand.

The Bible tells us

Do not repay anyone evil for evil, be careful to do what is right in the eyes of everyone.

Romans 12:17, NIV

As our former First Lady Michelle Obama Said. *"When they go low, we go high."*

The Bible tells us

Let us not become weary in doing good. For at the proper time, we will reap a harvest if we do not give up.

Galatians 6:9

It also says

Do not fret because of those who do evil or those who do wrong, for like the grass they will soon wither like green plants they will soon die away.

Psalms 37 1-2, NIV

Most of our forefathers never fought to get the upper hand, they only fought to be treated equally. Therefore, if no one else does what is right, no matter what others are doing, we must continue to do what is right in the eyes of God. This is how spiritual battles are won!

Christ is in Control

Without Christ at the forefront of our battles, if we are not careful, we can get so involved with the fighting itself and become so emotional about a cause, that the very things we are fighting against, we can also get caught up or tangled up ourselves. And I repeat, the very people we are fighting against to change their ways, we can become.

How can we accuse someone of being a racist if we don't admit that we too can possess the potential of becoming racist, with the attitude, "You hate me? I will hate you right back." In a sense, we can leave God out and make the fight about us and not about seeking righteousness. We can think we are doing right but it turns out to be for all the wrong reasons.

For example, some of us have had a run-in with police. Some have been treated so unfairly by those few that it caused many of us to lump the whole justice system into one unit, assuming that all police and public officials are terrible, which is so far from the truth. There is good and bad in all walks of life, professions, and all people.

Let's look at Paul, though He was a Roman citizen, it did not stop him from being a victim of religious leaders through the Roman system, yet his life was also saved by that same Roman system. In Acts 21:27-40 Paul was a victim of extremists who accused him of breaching a certain barricade that only Jews were allowed to enter the temple. Paul indeed ministered to the Gentiles, however, when he entered the temple, the extremists assumed that Paul brought the Gentiles with him, which in their way of thinking, contaminated the temple.

This was a law that Romans allowed and for the Jewish religious leader's authority to enforce to anyone who broke this law up to execution. The extremists, who caused a huge uproar, while taking Paul into custody, started beating him seeking to kill him. News reached the Commander of the Roman troops that the whole city of Jerusalem was in an uproar. He quickly took officers with him and ran to the crowd. When the rioters saw the Commander and his soldiers, they stopped beating Paul.

The Commander had taken Paul into their custody, bound him thinking he was the Egyptian who was usually causing an uproar among the citizens. When they were beginning to flog and interrogate him, Paul made it known that he was a Roman citizen, and the interrogation immediately stopped.

The point is that the same system that he was at times the victim of is the same system that saved his life. This lets us know that no matter how corrupt we feel a system could be, God is in control. Do we remember Nebuchadnezzar, King of Babylon, when he tried to take credit for what God had built through him?

He was walking on the roof of his palace in Babylon when he said in so many words with great pride. I built this kingdom with my might, my power, my strength. Immediately he was stricken with insanity for seven years until he looked up and acknowledged that God is God. God is in control no matter how things may appear. He is the ultimate authority. Nebuchadnezzar even learned that!

In Romans 13, it speaks about how all authority comes from God. Although we have corrupt leaders, God still has the upper hand and will deal with those leaders. However, it gives us no right to take the law into our own hands and disrespect all authority. Although America is not perfect and has many flaws, so far, we have the best judicial system in the world. If it were not for it, America would tear itself apart.

Again, the bible tells us:

> **Do not fret because of those who are evil or envious
> of those who do wrong**

Psalms 37:1, NIV

> **Like the green grass, they will soon
> wither. Like the green plants,
> they will soon die.**

Psalms 37:2, NIV

Let's not desire to do what is wrong as the world does to make things right.

Again, the bible also tells us:

> **Let us not become weary in doing good,
> for in proper time we will reap a harvest
> if we do not give up.**

Galatians 6:9, NIV

We can't do what the world does to get the blessings that God desires us to have. When Israel became a nation, they began to enter idol worshipping because it looked as though the pagan nations were doing great without God and seemed to be prospering.

As a result, Israel started intermingling and adopting their ways and even started worshipping their idols. They stopped depending on God as their deliverer and looked to the same nations that oppressed them such as Assyria and Egypt for help when other nations were attacking them.

We as people of color left our first love, just as in Israel we started looking at other resources outside of God, we started depending on and beholding other resources outside of God ourselves such as political parties, individuals with swelling promises, and organizations. This is not to say that we should not vote or participate in organizations.

Please, I encourage all to vote and live and enjoy the Lord and His works, however, if we are not careful, we start looking up to people who have power, prestige, and respect of the world but have no approval from God.

Most of us look for them to solve all our problems for us, thinking if we place them in a place of authority, then all our problems will be over, every day will be Sunday, sabbath will have no end. Some were either in the office or had a position of power that we placed on pedestals, assuming they could move the world. As soon as they don't fulfill all our needs or wants, we tend to listen or move to others who can tickle our ears or lick our wounds.

Anything that sounds feels good or looks good we are quickly caught up and deceived by the first whim that comes our way. This is what can cause division, especially among people of color because, without God, we are so vulnerable and tender at heart. We depend on the system to help us but in the same breath, we swear that the system has hurt us.

As inconsistent as the system is, just as Israel depended on Egypt to fight their battles, we still depend on the system or the government alone to help us. Let me make this clear, God is sovereign and has complete control over the government, no matter who is running it, good or bad. But when we depend on the government through our philosophical views or our religion based on how God should work for us or through us, this causes division, deep heated arguments, hatred, envy, strife and always looking down on others to get ahead.

Praying for our government or our leaders as the bible says is left on the back burner of our minds. I was talking to someone one day when President Trump was in office. I made the statement that I may not agree with him, but he needs our prayers. I was quickly rebuffed and ridiculed simply because I said he needed prayer.

When President Biden became president, I made a statement to pray for him, I was told "How can you be a Christian or a Pastor and pray for Joe Biden? Though this was not someone of color who made this statement, we as people of color have always learned to pray for all our leaders no matter who is in office, but now because we have somewhat of a voice, we have joined the ranks of the world by trying to control who to pray for and who not to pray for.

The very things that we have fought against, we are slowly becoming. It's no longer about Jesus or the church, it's about politics, power, money, prestige, and respect. These traits are now running the church. The evidence is in the falling away.

It's Time to Come Back Home

God is calling people of color home now. He is telling us to come back to our first love. Come back to where we first believed, come back to where He first freed us, come back to where He first revealed Himself to us, and come back to where we first inspired others to come to Jesus and see him for who He is. Come back to where we were weak yet through Him, we were strong.

As simple as this may sound, it's difficult for some of us people of color to comprehend the fact that all our help comes from God! We can get so caught up in this world and its deceptions that even simple scriptures such as

For what shall it profit a man to gain the whole world and lose his soul?

Mark 8:34-38, NIV

Or what a man gives in exchange for his soul after a while makes no sense to us. For some of us, it's not about a fair shake or just being treated equally anymore, it's about having our power. Having our prestige, having our respect, yet we ask, where is God?

When we start depending on our wisdom, knowledge, and leaning to our understanding, or as the bible says, building our house on the sand, it may stand for a little while but eventually, it will fall. In other words, we can build on our philosophical views, winning cleaver arguments, but it will not last.

Today, we as people of color and those who share our burdens, are like Ezekiel 37:1-14 describing Israel as dry bones. The Lord brought Ezekiel to the valley of Dry Bones. As he began to wonder why he was there, the Lord, asked Ezekiel, "What do you see?" He replied, "I see very dry bones. They have no life, separated from one another." The Lord asked, "Can these dry bones live again?"

After a conversation about the bones being dry, with no hope of coming together, the Lord told Ezekiel to prophesy to these bones. As he began to prophesy, the bones began to come together and added skin. Though the bones had come together, Ezekiel noticed that the bones were still dead and there was no life.

Remember when the Lord formed Adam out of the dust of the earth? There was no life in the body.

When God blew into the body of Adam, he became a living soul. As the Lord also blew the breath of life into Adam, He did the same to the bones when Ezekiel prophesied to them, and they became a living army.

The book of Acts speaks of the disciples in the upper room in Jerusalem where they were to meet, waiting for the Holy Spirit to come down and empower them for the works of Christ. Before this meeting, Jesus taught, and ministered to them the truths about who He was and encouraged them to spread the good news to others.

We all know the story of how Judas betrayed Him. Peter denied Him, and the rest of the disciples deserted Him and became scattered (Christ Himself told them not to follow Him). He was then crucified for the sins of the whole world. Early Sunday morning, Jesus got up out of the grave and declared victory over sin death, and the grave.

For forty days, Jesus appeared to the Disciples at different times, encouraging them, and bringing them together preparing for His departure. They had no idea where Christ was going with this. All they knew was before He went up, He told them to wait on the comforter in the upper room in Jerusalem.

The day that they went to the upper room, they were all together in one accord, they seemed stagnated, a little lost and I believe it's safe to say, no life. Not knowing what to expect.

However, the spirit came down like fire. It had the sound of a rushing wind bringing spiritual life, empowering them to not only speak in different languages, but it also empowered them to spread the gospel with boldness, assurance, and strength.

The evidence of the spirit was when the disciples began to spread the gospel. 3000 people were baptized, the lame walked, the blind could see, many were healed of diseases and those who were out of their minds were brought back into their right minds.

Amid the chaos, along with all the signs and wonders, there was so much joy, unity, and peace in the hearts of the people.

Though it seems that the world has gone into chaos, and we have allowed ourselves to get caught up, God is still looking to empower us today. However, there are complaints that we will not work together, nor will we help one another. Some of us have also allowed the world to affect us so much that will not speak to one another or hold simple conversations with one another, and for many trust is nonexistent for the fear of being used or taken advantage of.

There are complaints that some of us hate one another so much, that we hurt one another and at times even kill one another. There are complaints that we take from one another, deceive one another steal from one another, or gossip about one another so bad that it causes dysfunction among families and friends.

In all this chaos, as we walk around our families, our homes, our jobs, our schools, our friends and relatives, and even our churches. We see people who are so hurt or spiritually damaged that it affects them economically, socially, sociologically, emotionally, and at times mentally.

The Lord Jesus is asking us, as preachers, ministers, laymen, evangelists, and Christian folks, can these dry bones live again? Can life be restored, can we come together? Can these dry bones live? With all the hurt and pain that's so deep, that healing would seem impossible, God continues to ask the question, can these dry bones live?

When trust is almost nonexistent, to where we can't or will not forgive, when we continue to fight over small issues that become big issues and solving them would seem all uphill, while we are asking the Lord what's going on? He is asking us can these dry bones live.

As we continue to scratch our heads and twiddle of thumbs, we notice there is a silence. The Lord Jesus is not giving any answers, however, He is telling us "Prophesy to these cold dry bones of ours". Stop complaining and prophecy. Stop burying our heads in the sand and act as though spiritual stagnation does not exist and prophesy.

Stop hiding behind the Church, trying to justify our sins through working different programs where competition with one another is such a priority that the works of the Lord are placed on the back burner. God is telling us to prophesy to these dry bones!

If we start speaking, start prophesying to the people around us, we will be surprised to see how spiritually hungry people are today. Most people today want to hear a word from the Lord. As we start speaking and the people become attentive, God will start blowing.

As God starts blowing, new life will be resurrected, hearts will soften, darkness will turn to light, and attitudes will change from negative to positive. People can begin to speak and care for one another, encourage one another, and even learn to pray for one another.

Now is the time to make up our minds and come back to our first love. Come back to where we first believed. Today is not the time to stand at a crossroads of indecisiveness, wondering where we fit in. If we take the initial step and come back to God, placing total trust in Him, He will show us and empower us with a fresh spirit. Yes!

That same spirit that empowered the disciples during the time of Pentecost can still empower us today in new ways. In other words, the spirit has not changed, it just needs to be refreshed in our lives in a new way. Through the spirit, we can be restored, recharged, and renewed. Yes! I can hear the old preacher saying, He gave me a new walk and a new talk. He reestablished my comings and my goings. He gave me purpose and reason for living for Him.

With a fresh new way of receiving the spirit, we receive joy in our hearts. We can love when we felt we could not love before. We can forgive when we feel that forgiveness is impossible. We can endure trials, tribulations, heartaches, and pains knowing that The Lord Jesus will use them to strengthen and build our character; to equip us to inspire and be a help to others.

With this same spirit we can be refreshed in new ways to where we can't help but declare to all whom we meet, that Jesus is my Alpha and Omega, He's my beginning He's, my end. He's my First, He's My last. He's my bright morning star. He is my bread when I'm hungry, my water when I'm thirsty. He's my wheel in the middle of a wheel, He's my Rose of Sharon. This will affect our attitude in such a way that we can't help but praise him because He's been too good!

WORKS CITED

Evans, Tony. *Discover Your Destiny: Let God Use You Like He Made You.* Harvest House Publishers, 2013.

Montalvo, D. G., & Magl, M. (Eds.). *Tyler's History of White Supremacy.* People First Framework, 2021. Edited by Tina Bausinger.

NIV (New International Version) Study Bible. Zondervan, 2002.

Powe, F. Douglas. *New Wine New Wine Skins.* The United Methodist Publishing House, 2012.

The Poem P.U.S.H Pray Until Something Happens. The author is unknown.

Wiersbe, Warren W. *The Wiersbe Bible Commentary.* David C. Cook, Publisher, 2003.

Don't miss out!

Visit the website below and you can sign up to receive emails whenever Leonard Spurling publishes a new book. There's no charge and no obligation.

https://books2read.com/r/B-A-ZOMWB-IAROE

BOOKS 2 READ

Connecting independent readers to independent writers.